ROBOTS EXPLORING SPACE

DAWN PROBE

A Robot Explores the Dwarf Planet Ceres

James Bow

PowerKiDS
press™

NEW YORK

Published in 2017 by **The Rosen Publishing Group**
29 East 21st Street, New York, NY 10010

Produced for Rosen by Calcium

Editors for Calcium: Sarah Eason and Harriet McGregor
Designers for Calcium: Jennie Child
Picture researcher: Rachel Blount

Picture credits: Cover: NASA/JPL (Dawn Probe image), Getty Images: Ron Miller/Stocktrek Images
(Ceres image), Thinkstock: Pixtum (top banner), Shutterstock: Andrey_Kuzmin (metal plate),
Thinkstock: -strizh- (back cover illustration); Inside: NASA: JPL/Orbital Sciences Corporation 14,
JPL-Caltech 13, 19, 20, 23, 29, JPL-Caltech/UCLA/MPS/DLR/IDA 24, 27; Wikimedia Commons:
Background- William K. Hartmann, Courtesy of UCLA; image-NASA/MCREL 10, NASA 17, NASA/
JPL-Caltech 5, 6-7, PlanetUser, Gregory H. Revera, NASA/JPL-Caltech/UCLA/MPS/DLR/IDA 9.

CATALOGING-IN-PUBLICATION DATA

Names: Bow, James.
Title: Dawn probe: a robot explores the dwarf planet Ceres / James Bow.
Description: New York : Powerkids Press, 2017. | Series: Robots exploring space | Includes index.
Identifiers: ISBN 9781508151319 (pbk.) | ISBN 9781508151258 (library bound) |
   ISBN 9781508151142 (6 pack)
Subjects: LCSH: Ceres (Dwarf planet)--Juvenile literature. | Space probes--Juvenile literature.
Classification: LCC QB653.V47 B69 2017 | DDC 523.44--dc23

Manufactured in the United States of America
CPSIA Compliance Information: Batch #BS16PK. For Further Information contact Rosen Publishing, New York, New York at 1-800-237-9932

CONTENTS

Robots in Space

Outer space is an amazing mystery. It has planets and moons that are like nothing we see on Earth, and yet they can teach us about our planet and how life formed on it. With the help of **robots**, humans are now discovering more about space than ever before.

While people have visited Earth's **orbit** and even walked on the moon, there are limits to how far they can go. People must take a lot of equipment with them when they go into space. They need air, water, and food, and space journeys are difficult. Space is massive and it takes a long time to travel through it. Robots do not need food, water, or air. They can **hibernate** as they journey to their space destination. When there, they can take pictures, scan and analyze objects, and communicate with people back on Earth.

New Frontiers

Thanks to robots, humans know a lot about the most distant planets in the solar system. However, space continues to surprise us, and it seems the more robots we send to explore it, the more questions we discover. This book focuses on a robot called the *Dawn* **probe,** and its mission to explore a part of space called the asteroid belt, between the orbits of Mars and Jupiter. In this part of space there are many small rocks, from which there is much to learn. They may even help us understand how our solar system was born.

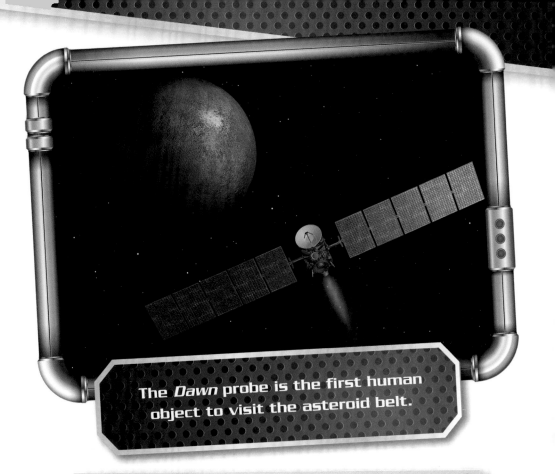

The *Dawn* probe is the first human object to visit the asteroid belt.

SPACE DISCOVERY

WHY DO PEOPLE SEND ROBOTS INTO SPACE? ROBOTS ARE MACHINES THAT CAN DO MANY DIFFERENT TASKS. A ROBOT HAS A COMPUTER BRAIN THAT CAN PERFORM DIFFERENT INSTRUCTIONS, DEPENDING ON THE SITUATION. THE FARTHER A SPACECRAFT IS FROM EARTH, THE LONGER IT TAKES FOR SIGNALS TO GET THERE. A MESSAGE FROM EARTH CAN TAKE 15–30 MINUTES TO REACH THE ASTEROID BELT, SO A SPACECRAFT REPORTING A PROBLEM MIGHT HAVE TO WAIT AN HOUR BEFORE GETTING INSTRUCTIONS ABOUT HOW TO FIX THE PROBLEM. HOWEVER, A SPACE ROBOT CAN MAKE A LOT OF PROBLEM-FIXING DECISIONS FOR ITSELF.

Asteroid or Planet?

Up to the late eighteenth century, scientists knew of only seven planets in our solar system: Mercury, Venus, Earth, Mars, Jupiter, Saturn, and Uranus. At the time, scientists took note of the unusually long distance between the orbits of Mars and Jupiter, and wondered if there might be a planet there. Astronomers started to search for it through their telescopes.

In 1801, astronomer Giuseppe Piazzi (1746–1826) found a dim object in the sky. He thought it was a small planet and named it Ceres, after the Roman goddess of the harvest. Because Neptune was not discovered until 1846, Ceres became our solar system's eighth planet.

Getting Crowded

However, 15 months after the discovery of Ceres, German astronomer Heinrich Olbers (1758–1840) discovered another planet in the same region. This was called Pellas. In 1807, another two planets were found, Juno and Vesta.

Astronomers asked how could four planets share the same orbit in space? When a fifth object, named Astraea, was discovered in 1845, astronomers decided that it was no longer right to call these objects planets. They were smaller than any other planet in the solar system, and more and more of them were being discovered. So astronomers created a new category of space object. Ceres, Pellas, Juno, Vesta, and Astraea were called **asteroids**, meaning "starlike." As more asteroids were discovered in the same region of space, the area became known as the asteroid belt.

This is an artist's depiction of an asteroid belt. In reality, the asteroids are millions of miles apart.

SPACE DISCOVERY

ASTEROIDS RANGE IN SIZE FROM A SPECK OF DUST TO OBJECTS HUNDREDS OF MILES ACROSS. MORE THAN 200 OBJECTS ARE KNOWN TO BE LARGER THAN 62 MILES (100 KM) WIDE! HALF THE **MASS** OF THE ASTEROID BELT IS CONTAINED IN THE FOUR LARGEST ASTEROIDS: CERES, VESTA, PELLAS, AND HYGIEA.

Groundwork for Dawn

When the National Aeronautics and Space Administration (NASA) launched the *Dawn* probe in September 2007, it was the result of years of planning and hard work. When the *Dawn* mission was announced in 2001, little was known about the asteroid belt. In 1995, the Hubble Space Telescope had taken photos of Ceres and found interesting features on its surface. However, asteroids are small and distant, so it is difficult to take clear images of them.

NASA scientists proposed the *Dawn* mission because it would explore an area of space that had not been visited by spacecraft. It would provide a closeup look at not just the largest asteroid in the asteroid belt, Ceres, but also another large asteroid, Vesta. Asteroids such as Vesta formed early in the history of the solar system, when dust clumped together to create larger objects that became planets. Asteroids stopped growing before they had a chance to become planets, so visiting Vesta and Ceres would be like visiting the early years of the solar system!

Many Targets

The *Dawn* mission had to compete for funding with other important projects, such as completing the International Space Station (ISS) and sending the *New Horizons* probe to Pluto. Between 2003 and 2006, the *Dawn* mission was canceled twice. It was only given the go ahead after *Dawn*'s manufacturer, Orbital Sciences Corporation, offered to sell the spacecraft to NASA for only the cost it took to build it.

SPACE DISCOVERY

In 1995, the Hubble Space Telescope found a mysterious dark spot on Ceres. It was thought to be a crater. The spot was named Piazzi in honor of the astronomer who had found Ceres. By looking at this spot, and other small spots, astronomers were able to figure out how fast Ceres is spinning and the length of its day (9 hours and 4 minutes).

This image shows the relative sizes of Ceres (top left), our moon (top right), and Earth (bottom).

Dwarf Planets

While NASA scientists worked on the *Dawn* probe, scientists again questioned whether Ceres was an asteroid or a planet. Though small by other planets' standards, Ceres was spherical, like a ball. Most asteroids have an irregular shape. There was also evidence that a **molten core**, an area of hot liquid rock, might have existed beneath Ceres' surface, making it more like a planet.

The Pluto Problem

The question about whether Ceres was a planet or an asteroid was partly caused by Pluto. In an area beyond Pluto, called the Kuiper belt, are many large icy and rocky objects. Some of these are larger

Dawn's mission to discover more about asteroids would help scientists classify, or group, these distant and mysterious objects.

than Pluto. The size of these objects made astronomers argue that they could be considered planets, too. And if these large objects could be planets, so could Ceres.

A Whole New Class

However, astronomers felt that Ceres and Pluto were too different from the eight larger planets in the solar system to be called planets. So, they added a new rule for planets, saying that they had to have cleared their orbit of other objects. Ceres and Pluto had not. As a result, in 2006, astronomers decided Pluto was no longer a planet. But, astronomers wanted to show that Pluto and Ceres were different from regular asteroids. To do this, they put Pluto and Ceres in a new category, "dwarf planets." As of 2016, five dwarf planets have been recognized in our solar system: Ceres, Pluto, Haumea, Makemake, and Eris. Ceres is the only dwarf planet in the asteroid belt.

SPACE DISCOVERY

THE ASTEROID BELT IS NOT THE REMAINS OF A PLANET THAT BLEW UP. INSTEAD, IT IS THE LEFTOVER REMAINS OF A DUST CLOUD THAT EXISTED WHEN OUR SOLAR SYSTEM WAS BORN, MORE THAN 5 BILLION YEARS AGO. AS DUST IN THE CLOUD CLUMPED TOGETHER TO FORM PLANETS, MARS AND JUPITER ATE UP SO MUCH OF THE DUST THAT NOT ENOUGH REMAINED IN THE ASTEROID BELT FOR A NEW PLANET TO FORM. INSTEAD, ASTEROIDS FORMED FROM THE REMAINING DUST, AND CERES GREW TO BE THE BIGGEST OF THEM ALL.

Planning

To investigate the asteroid belt, scientists designed a probe that would last the nine-year mission required. It was named *Dawn*. To build it, NASA turned to Orbital Sciences Corporation. Working with NASA's plans for the mission, Orbital Sciences set up the flight system and all the equipment the probe would need, called the scientific payload. Among the equipment was a very powerful camera, which could take images of Vesta and Ceres and send them back to Earth. The camera would also help *Dawn* navigate.

Loading the Science

As well as the camera, builders installed an **infrared** and visible light **spectrometer.** This would find and measure light reflected off of the asteroid's surface. By seeing how the light changed as it returned to the spectrometer, scientists would discover what the asteroid surface is made of. A similar device added to the spacecraft was a Gamma Ray and Neutron Detector (GRaND). This would be used to find particular atoms that were important for forming rocks and water.

Space First

Included on *Dawn* was an inch-long microchip containing the names of a number of people fascinated by space. The names were collected in 2006, before the launch, as more than 360,000 people wrote to NASA to have their names sent up into space.

The *Dawn* probe is managed by an onboard computer. It controls the equipment, and talks to **mission control** on Earth using one of two antennae. Two star trackers keep an eye on the position of known stars, to figure out the probe's position in the solar system and make changes to the **trajectory** if needed.

When it was put together, the *Dawn* probe weighed 2,370 pounds (1,240 kg). It was powered by a **solar array** that could generate 1,300 watts of power, even at three times the distance between Earth and the sun. With its solar array folded up, *Dawn* measured 7.7 feet (2.3 m). With the array extended, the probe was 65 feet (19.7 m) long.

Driving Dawn

The *Dawn* probe was the first spacecraft to explore the solar system with an **ion propulsion engine**. The engine works by using electricity to excite ions, which are atoms that have an **electric charge**. The electricity pushes these atoms out of the probe, which pushes the probe forward.

Spaceships need a lot of **thrust** to get out of Earth's gravity. This is usually provided by huge rockets that release a lot of energy. Once in space, spacecraft are weightless. They continue

This is an image of the ion propulsion engine installed on the *Dawn* probe.

ion thrusters

to move until a force acts against that movement. Before the ion propulsion engine, spaceships used quick rocket blasts to **accelerate** toward a planet. They then used the pull of the planet's gravity to accelerate again.

Ion Thrusters

Rocket fuel provides a lot of thrust in a short period of time. With ion propulsion, the amount of thrust is small compared to rockets. However, an ion engine can provide steady thrust over a much longer period of time, using less energy.

When *Dawn* launched in 2007, it had 937 pounds (425 kg) of xenon gas as fuel. *Dawn*'s three ion thrusters each release around 0.0001 ounces (3.25 mg) of xenon per second. This gives the probe enough xenon for more than 34 years of thrust. Scientists watched carefully to see how *Dawn*'s ion propulsion engine worked in space. If it worked well, it could later be used to build spacecraft that could carry robots to the outer solar system. It might one day be used to carry humans to Mars.

SPACE DISCOVERY

THE *DAWN* PROBE ALSO HAS REGULAR ROCKET THRUSTERS POWERED BY A FUEL CALLED HYDRAZINE. THIS IS A **MOLECULE** MADE OF HYDROGEN AND NITROGEN ATOMS. HYDRAZINE IS A VERY USEFUL SPACE FUEL. UNLIKE OTHER ROCKET FUELS, IT DOES NOT NEED OXYGEN TO BURN. HYDRAZINE IS EASILY STORED ON BOARD A SPACECRAFT. *DAWN*'S ROCKET THRUSTERS ARE USED TO TURN THE PROBE, ALLOWING IT TAKE A BETTER LOOK AT AN OBJECT IN SPACE.

Countdown to Launch

With the *Dawn* probe built and ready to go, it arrived at Cape Canaveral, Florida, on April 10, 2007. However, *Dawn*'s launch did not go according to plan. The probe was due to be launched into space on June 20. However, problems delayed the launch. First, important parts were not received on time, and the launch was held back until June 30. Then, a broken crane at the launch pad delayed the launch again, to July 7. However, on this date bad weather delayed the launch a third time.

Schedule Conflict

The launch had to be suspended once more because another spacecraft needed the launch pad. NASA launched the *Phoenix* mission to Mars, and a new launch date for *Dawn* was planned for September 26. However, bad weather again caused another delay.

On September 27, just when *Dawn* was ready to go, the countdown was stopped because a boat accidentally entered the exclusion area in the ocean off the coast of Cape Canaveral! This area was the place where booster rockets from the launch were expected to crash, so NASA had to wait until the boat was safely escorted out of harm's way.

Finally, at 7:34 a.m. on September 27, 2007, NASA counted down and the rocket carrying the *Dawn* probe soared into the sky. *Dawn* at last began its journey to the asteroid belt.

SPACE DISCOVERY

THE DELAYS TO THE LAUNCH OF DAWN WERE A BIG CONCERN. EARTH AND CERES ARE NOT SIMPLY STANDING STILL IN SPACE, THEY ARE BOTH **ORBITING** AROUND THE SUN. THIS MEANS THAT AT DIFFERENT TIMES EARTH IS MUCH CLOSER TO CERES THAN AT OTHER TIMES. THE BEST TIME TO LAUNCH WAS WHILE THE DISTANCE BETWEEN EARTH AND CERES WAS BECOMING SMALLER. THIS PERIOD OF TIME WAS CALLED THE LAUNCH WINDOW. THE ACTION OF EARTH MOVING TOWARD CERES WOULD PROVIDE A SPEED BOOST FOR DAWN AND MEAN IT WOULD TAKE LESS TIME AND FUEL TO TRAVEL TO CERES.

NASA launches rocke
from Cape Canavera
(seen from space, her
because Earth's rotati
sends rockets east, ov
the ocean and away fr
people's homes.

Traveling to Vesta

Once *Dawn* escaped Earth's orbit, its ion thrusters took over. After some tests, the thrusters pushed the probe on its way. The thrusters gave *Dawn* more than 270 days of journey time, between December 17, 2007, and October 31, 2008. During that time, the *Dawn* probe accelerated to a speed of 1.12 miles (1.81 km) per second.

However, the *Dawn* probe needed another boost. To get this boost, on February 17, 2009, *Dawn* visited Mars. Passing just 341 miles (549 km) from the planet's surface, the probe used the pull of Mars's gravity to speed it up on its way to the asteroid belt. Two years later, on July 16, 2011, the *Dawn* probe arrived at its first asteroid, Vesta.

SPACE DISCOVERY

WHEN SPACECRAFT USE PLANETS FOR A "GRAVITY ASSIST," THEY USE THE PULL OF THE PLANET'S GRAVITY AND ITS MOVEMENT THROUGH SPACE. THIS HELPS SPACECRAFT SPEED UP, IN THE SAME WAY THAT A SLOW ROLLER-SKATER PULLING AGAINST A SPEEDING ROLLER-SKATER SPEEDS UP. JUST AS THIS ACTION SLOWS DOWN THE SPEEDING ROLLER-SKATER, DAWN SLOWED MARS DOWN. THANKS TO DAWN, MARS WILL END UP ABOUT 1 INCH (2.3 CM) AWAY FROM ITS USUAL POSITION IN ORBIT OVER THE NEXT 180 MILLION YEARS.

Vesta is 330 miles (531 km) in diameter and takes 1,325 Earth days to orbit around the sun.

Dry Vesta

Vesta was chosen for a visit because it was so different from Ceres. Ceres has been called a "wet asteroid," but Vesta is "dry." It has no signs of water or ice. *Dawn* moved into orbit around Vesta and between August 2011 and September 2012, it studied the asteroid from different **altitudes**.

Dawn's studies of Vesta suggested that the asteroid had a metal-rich core. The probe also explored a gigantic crater, named the Rheasilvia crater, on Vesta's south pole. At 295 miles (475 km) in diameter and 8 miles (13 km) deep, the crater was caused when a meteor smashed into the asteroid. This smash moved more than 239,99 cubic miles (1 million cubic km) of rock on Vesta's surface. That is enough rock to fill the Grand Canyon 1,000 times!

Working Around Failure

Dawn was supposed to leave Vesta on August 26, 2012. Unfortunately, a problem with one of the probe's reaction wheels caused a delay. The reaction wheel helps turn the probe while in orbit. Although the probe could still leave Vesta, NASA kept it in orbit until September 5, 2012, so they could look at the problem. While they could not fix it, they were able to figure out a way to turn the probe. They combined the power of the remaining reaction wheels with the ion drive to turn the probe.

Most ion thrusters use xenon gas as their fuel, which is safe to handle. However, *Dawn* did encounter problems with its ion thrusters.

It is not easy to fix a problem with a probe in space. There is no way NASA can send a repair team into space! Instead, NASA scientists have to think about what they have available on the spacecraft itself, and how they can use that to fix or work around the problem. Sometimes, moving an instrument in a certain way can help. Other times, equipment on the spacecraft has to take over to do the job of the damaged machine.

Safe Mode

On September 11, 2014, *Dawn*'s ion thruster stopped firing, and the probe put itself in "safe mode." NASA designed the probe to shut down all nonessential systems when it found a problem, to protect instruments and equipment from harm. When *Dawn* entered safe mode, the mission team switched to a backup thruster while they looked at the problem. They later decided that a controller on the ion drive may have been damaged by a **high-energy particle**, and only needed to be started up again. On September 15, 2014, NASA sent a signal to take *Dawn* out of safe mode. The probe's original ion thruster started working again properly, and *Dawn* continued on its journey to Ceres.

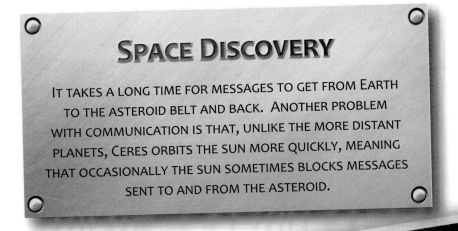

SPACE DISCOVERY

It takes a long time for messages to get from Earth to the asteroid belt and back. Another problem with communication is that, unlike the more distant planets, Ceres orbits the sun more quickly, meaning that occasionally the sun sometimes blocks messages sent to and from the asteroid.

Arrival At Ceres

To get from Vesta to Ceres, the *Dawn* probe had to travel 900 million miles (1.5 billion km). That is more than half the distance *Dawn* had already traveled to get from Earth to Vesta. *Dawn* got close enough to start photographing Ceres on December 1, 2014. It finally entered the asteroid's orbit on March 6, 2015.

The *Dawn* probe went through several orbits at different altitudes to get a good look at Ceres. Between March 6 and April 23, 2015, *Dawn* orbited above the dwarf planet's poles, scanning the surface. It created a map of the shape of Ceres' surface.

Between April 23 and May 9, *Dawn* lowered itself to an orbit 8,400 miles (13,520 km) from the surface of Ceres. It started to take detailed pictures of the landscape, and analyzed the chemistry of the rocks using its infrared spectrometer. From May 9 to June 6, *Dawn* slowly began to spiral down to 2,700 miles (4,345 km) from the surface to make more detailed maps and carry out analysis.

Back on Earth

NASA scientists received **data** from *Dawn*, and kept an eye on the spacecraft to be ready should any problems occur. On June 30, the *Dawn* probe had a problem with its software that caused it to go into safe mode again. Engineers investigated and figured out that there was a problem with one of the probe's three ion engines. Fortunately, they could switch to one of the other ion engines and they decided that *Dawn* could continue without the faulty engine.

Orbiting Ceres, *Dawn* was now 257 million miles (414 million km) from the sun.

Mysteries of Ceres

Even before arriving at Ceres, the *Dawn* mission was uncovering things about the dwarf planet that fascinated scientists. Bright spots were discovered on the surface of Ceres, and scientists could only guess what they were. They were four times brighter than the surrounding areas. Were they ice? Was this proof that there was water beneath the surface of Ceres? Scientists looked forward to finding out.

Looking at Ceres

Between June 6 and June 30, the *Dawn* probe orbited 2,750 miles (4,426 km) from the surface of Ceres, scanning the entire surface of the dwarf planet every three Earth days. The probe's infrared

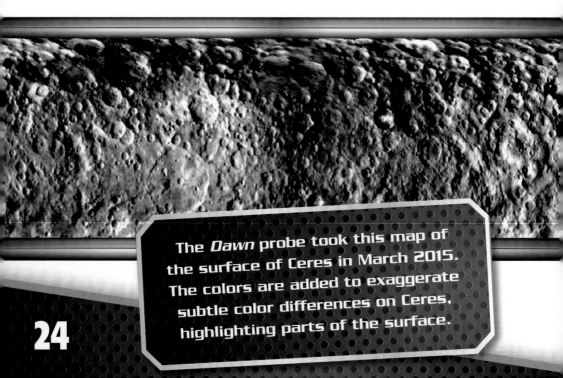

The *Dawn* probe took this map of the surface of Ceres in March 2015. The colors are added to exaggerate subtle color differences on Ceres, highlighting parts of the surface.

spectrometers began to make detailed analysis of the surface. Between June 30 and August 17, the *Dawn* probe lowered itself even farther, to just 920 miles (1,481 km) from the surface of Ceres. There it took its most detailed photographs yet. Finally, on October 23, *Dawn* dropped to its fourth and final orbit, just 233 miles (375 km) from the surface. There, its GRaND would begin its chemical analysis of the planet.

The *Dawn* mission was set to officially end in 2016. Some thought was given to visiting the asteroid Pellas after the Ceres mission was complete. However, the position of Pellas compared to Ceres meant that *Dawn* could only fly past the asteroid and not orbit it. It was decided instead to make *Dawn* become a permanent satellite to Ceres, orbiting it like an artificial moon. By doing so, *Dawn* will keep watch on the closest dwarf planet from Earth.

Amazing Ceres

 Though the Herschel Space Observatory discovered water before *Dawn* arrived, the probe could look closer and provide a better idea of how much water was beneath Ceres's surface. Were the bright spots on the planet salts left behind as water spewed out from the surface of the dwarf planet? Or were they "ice rinks?" Scientists do not yet know for sure, and have to look at the data before they can come to a conclusion.

 Scientists do think that Ceres has an icy mantle. This is a thick layer of ice miles beneath the surface, with possibly an ocean of liquid fresh water trapped beneath the ice. This ocean may contain more fresh water than all the fresh water of Earth!

Amazing Vesta

Vesta was found to have surprises of its own. While in orbit, the *Dawn* probe discovered signs of ancient volcanic eruptions. It found a mountain on Vesta's south pole that was bigger than

SPACE DISCOVERY

The asteroid belt contains a lot of precious metals such as nickel, iron, and titanium, which makes it attractive to ambitious miners. However, the most precious resource there is water. Not only can we drink water, but we can change it into oxygen and hydrogen for use as rocket fuel. This could make Ceres a good fuel stop for deep-space spacecraft.

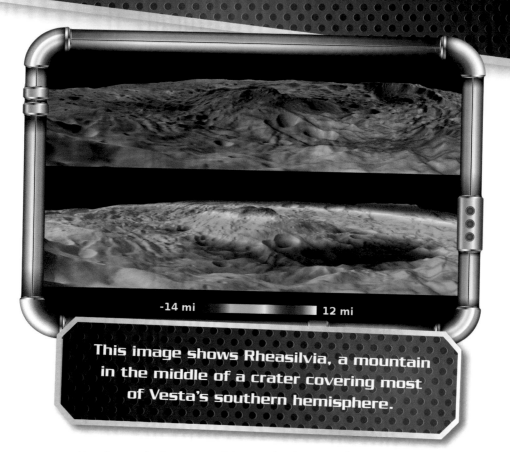

-14 mi ▭ 12 mi

This image shows Rheasilvia, a mountain in the middle of a crater covering most of Vesta's southern hemisphere.

any on Earth, and almost as big as the huge Olympus Mons volcano on Mars. The eruptions from Vesta's volcanoes have created a crust on the southern hemisphere that is only 1–2 billion years old. This is far younger than the crust of Vesta's northern hemisphere. This tells scientists that the volcanoes on Vesta's southern hemisphere have been erupting for some time, and constantly renewing the surface.

The data that *Dawn* collects is sent back to Earth through the probe's antennae. The distance between Earth and Ceres makes the data connection between *Dawn* and NASA slow. It takes 1–2 minutes to fully download a single photograph. Thousands of photographs and a lot of data have to be sent to Earth, so scientists have some time to wait before all the data comes back.

The Mission Continues

From 2016, the *Dawn* probe will operate only as a satellite orbiting Ceres, but for the scientists behind the mission, the work will continue. The *Dawn* probe took many pictures, and gathered a huge amount of data. It will take years for scientists to examine it all and see how it explains the mysteries of the asteroid belt. Already major discoveries have been made, such as the presence of water and the activity of Vesta's volcanoes. Who knows what other discoveries await?

Robots in Space!

Thanks to *Dawn*, scientists learned more about the asteroid belt than would have been possible had a spacecraft gone out with a human crew to examine the belt. The work that robots have carried out to explore space has pushed back the boundaries of our knowledge, and revealed exciting possibilities for future missions.

However, we must not forget that every robot in space is backed by dozens of scientists, astronomers, and engineers, who put the probes together, plan their journeys, monitor the mission, and examine the data that is uncovered. It is the working partnership between robots and people that expands our knowledge, and makes people on Earth just as important to these discoveries as the robots in space.

SPACE DISCOVERIES

Dawn may not be alone on Ceres for long. The Chinese Space Agency is planning a mission to the dwarf planet. Sometime in the 2020s, a robot lander could reach the surface of Ceres, gather material, and bring it back to Earth. In the far future, Ceres could even be a stopping point for spacecraft to refuel, so they can extend their trips to the outer solar system.

By looking at Ceres and Vesta, we can look back at the start of the solar system, when objects like these asteroids crashed together to eventually make planets.

accelerate To speed up.

altitudes Distances from the surface.

antennae Devices that send and receive radio signals.

asteroids Lumps of rock in space. Many orbit the sun in a band between Mars and Jupiter.

atmosphere A layer of gases that surround a planet or moon.

data Information.

electric charge A property of matter; a particle can have a positive or a negative charge.

hibernate To be in a state in which all nonessential systems in a spacecraft are switched off temporarily to save energy.

high-energy particle A small piece of matter carrying a lot of energy, like an X-ray.

infrared A form of light invisible to the human eye, with a longer wavelength and less energy than red light.

ion propulsion engine An engine that uses ions (atoms with an electrical charge) to push a spacecraft along.

mass The amount of matter that makes up an object.

mission control Scientists, technicians, and other people in charge of a space mission.

molecule The smallest amount of a chemical compound that can exist.

molten core A part of a planet deep beneath its surface where pressure and heat turns the rock into a liquid.

orbit A circular path around a space object.

orbiting Traveling around an object in a circular way.

probe A robot that is programmed to explore a particular area of space.

robots Machines that are programmed to carry out particular jobs.

solar array A lot of solar power cells grouped together to catch sunlight and turn it into electricity.

spectrometer A machine that identifies the makeup of an object by seeing how it interacts with light.

thrust Push.

trajectory Route taken by a moving object.

FOR MORE INFORMATION

Books

Furstinger, Nancy. *Robots in Space* (Lightning Bolt Books).
     Minneapolis, MN: Lerner Publications, 2014.

Greve, Tom. *Thanks, NASA!* (Let's Explore Science).
     North Mankato, MN: Rourke Educational Media, 2013.

Kortenkamp, Steve. *The Dwarf Planets* (The Solar System
     and Beyond). Mankato, MN: Capstone, 2011.

O'Hearn, Michael. *Awesome Space Robots*. Mankato, MN:
     Capstone, 2013.

Websites

Due to the changing nature of Internet links, PowerKids Press has
developed an online list of websites related to the subject of this
book. This site is updated regularly. Please use this link to access
the list: **www.powerkidslinks.com/res/dawn**

INDEX